iOS 18
A Deep Dive into AI - Unlocking All You Need to Know

Exploring Apple's Groundbreaking Update, Artificial Intelligence Enhancements, and the Future of Mobile Computing

Tech University

All rights reserved. No part of this publication may be reproduced, distributed, or transmitted in any form or by any means, including photocopying, recording, or other electronic or mechanical methods, without the prior written permission of the publisher, except in the case of brief quotations embodied in critical reviews and certain other noncommercial uses permitted by copyright law.

Copyright © Tech University, 2024.

Table of contents

Chapter 1: Introduction to iOS 18............................... 3
Chapter 2: The AI Revolution...................................... 6
Chapter 3: Unveiling iOS 18...................................... 14
Chapter 4: Siri: The Ultimate Virtual Assistant........ 24
Chapter 5: Redefining User Experience................... 35
Chapter 6: Enhancements in Built-in Apps...............45
Chapter 7: The Future of Messaging: RCS
Integration.. 57
Chapter 8: Accessibility and Inclusivity................... 64
Chapter 9: The Road Ahead...................................... 75
Conclusion.. 85

Chapter 1: Introduction to iOS 18

In a world where technology evolves at a relentless pace, one name stands at the forefront of innovation: Apple. For decades, this tech giant has captivated the world with its groundbreaking products, shaping the way we live, work, and connect with one another. And now, with the release of iOS 18, Apple is set to revolutionize the mobile landscape once again.

But what makes iOS 18 so special? What sets it apart from its predecessors and competitors alike? To answer these questions, we must first understand the driving force behind Apple's relentless pursuit of excellence: artificial intelligence.

From its humble beginnings to its current status as a global powerhouse, Apple has always been at the cutting edge of AI and machine learning. With each new iteration of its operating system, Apple has pushed the boundaries of what's possible, leveraging AI to enhance user experiences, streamline workflows, and unlock new levels of creativity.

And now, with iOS 18, Apple is poised to take AI to new heights. From Siri's newfound conversational prowess to the redesigned Home Screen and everything in between, iOS 18 represents the culmination of years of research, development, and innovation.

But this book isn't just about the features and functionalities of iOS 18. It's about the journey that led us here, the challenges we've overcome, and the endless possibilities that lie ahead. It's about exploring the intersection of technology and humanity, and the role that AI plays in shaping our collective future.

So join me as we embark on a journey into the heart of iOS 18. From its humble beginnings to its future potential, this book will be your guide to unlocking the full power of Apple's latest masterpiece. So sit back, relax, and prepare to be amazed. The future is here, and it's called iOS 18.

Chapter 2: The AI Revolution

In today's fast-paced world, artificial intelligence (AI) has become the driving force behind many technological advancements. From virtual assistants like Siri and Alexa to self-driving cars and personalized recommendations on streaming platforms, AI is ubiquitous in our daily lives, often operating behind the scenes, seamlessly enhancing our experiences without us even realizing it.

At its core, AI is about creating machines that can perform tasks that would typically require human intelligence. This includes understanding natural language, recognizing patterns in data, and making decisions based on that information. And as technology continues to evolve, so too does the role of AI in shaping our future.

One of the most significant areas where AI has made its mark is in improving efficiency and productivity. In industries like healthcare, finance, and manufacturing, AI-powered systems can analyze vast amounts of data in real-time, helping professionals make better decisions faster than ever before. This not only saves time and resources but also has the potential to save lives.

But AI isn't just about efficiency—it's also about creativity and innovation. In fields like art, music, and design, AI algorithms are being used to generate new ideas, push the boundaries of what's possible, and even collaborate with human creators to produce truly groundbreaking work.

However, with great power comes great responsibility. As AI becomes more advanced and integrated into our lives, questions about ethics, privacy, and control become increasingly important. How do we ensure that AI systems are fair and unbiased? How do we protect sensitive data from falling into the wrong hands? And perhaps most importantly, how do we ensure that AI is used for the benefit of humanity as a whole?

These are the questions that we must grapple with as we continue to harness the power of AI to shape the future of technology. And as we delve deeper into the role of artificial intelligence in modern society, one thing becomes clear: the possibilities are endless, and the only limit is our imagination.

Apple's investment in AI research and development

Apple's investment in artificial intelligence (AI) research and development is not just a recent endeavor but a long-standing commitment that has shaped the company's trajectory over the years. While Apple has always been synonymous with cutting-edge technology and innovative design, its emphasis on AI has become increasingly pronounced in recent years, reflecting a strategic shift towards harnessing the power of machine learning to enhance its products and services.

At the heart of Apple's AI initiatives lies a dedicated team of researchers, engineers, and data scientists who are pushing the boundaries of what's possible in the field of artificial intelligence. With a focus on both fundamental research and real-world applications, this team is responsible for developing the AI algorithms and technologies that power some of Apple's most iconic products, from the iPhone and iPad to Siri and Apple Watch.

But Apple's investment in AI goes beyond just developing new features and functionalities for its existing products. It's also about building the infrastructure and tools needed to support AI-driven innovation on a massive scale. This includes investments in hardware, such as the Neural Engine—a specialized chip designed specifically for accelerating machine learning tasks—and software, such as Core ML—a framework that makes it easy for developers to integrate machine learning models into their apps.

In addition to its internal research and development efforts, Apple has also made strategic acquisitions and partnerships to bolster its AI capabilities. From acquiring companies like Turi and VocalIQ to partnering with research institutions like Carnegie Mellon University, Apple is actively seeking out opportunities to collaborate with the best and brightest minds in the field of AI.

But perhaps the most telling sign of Apple's commitment to AI is the sheer magnitude of its investment. According to reports, Apple is spending more than $1 billion per year on AI research and development, making it one of the largest players in the industry. And with CEO Tim Cook himself touting AI as a top priority for the company, it's clear that Apple sees artificial intelligence not just as a technology, but as a fundamental driver of its future success.

In summary, Apple's investment in AI research and development is a testament to its unwavering commitment to innovation and excellence. By harnessing the power of machine learning, Apple is not only enhancing its products and services but also shaping the future of technology in ways we can only begin to imagine.

The potential impact of AI on iOS 18's features and Functionalities

The potential impact of artificial intelligence (AI) on iOS 18's features and functionalities is profound, promising to elevate the user experience to new heights and transform the way we interact with our devices. From intelligent personal assistants to enhanced app functionalities, AI integration in iOS 18 holds the key to unlocking a world of possibilities.

One of the most significant areas where AI is poised to make an impact is in enhancing user interactions with Siri, Apple's virtual assistant. With advanced natural language processing capabilities and machine learning algorithms, Siri in iOS 18 is expected to become more intuitive and responsive than ever before. Users can anticipate improved conversational abilities, allowing for more fluid and natural interactions with Siri across various tasks, from setting reminders and sending messages to controlling smart home devices.

Furthermore, AI-powered enhancements in iOS 18 will extend beyond Siri to various built-in apps and system functionalities. For example, the Photos app could leverage AI algorithms to automatically organize and categorize photos based on content, location, and time, making it easier for users to find and relive their favorite memories. Similarly, the Camera app may utilize AI-driven features such as scene recognition and intelligent composition suggestions to help users capture stunning photos effortlessly.

In addition to improving user interactions and app functionalities, AI in iOS 18 is also expected to play a significant role in enhancing device performance and efficiency. With features like on-device AI processing and optimization, iOS 18 can deliver faster app launch times, smoother multitasking, and improved battery life, ensuring a seamless and responsive user experience across the board.

Moreover, AI integration in iOS 18 opens up exciting possibilities for developers to create innovative and intelligent apps that leverage machine learning capabilities. With frameworks like Core ML and Create ML, developers can easily integrate AI models into their apps to deliver personalized recommendations, intelligent automation, and immersive experiences tailored to individual user preferences and behaviors.

Overall, the potential impact of AI on iOS 18's features and functionalities is vast and multifaceted, promising to revolutionize the way we interact with our devices and unlock new levels of productivity, creativity, and convenience. As iOS 18 continues to evolve and mature, users can look forward to a future where their devices are not just tools but intelligent companions that anticipate their needs, enhance their experiences, and empower them to do more than ever before.

Chapter 3: Unveiling iOS 18

In iOS 18, Apple introduces a slew of groundbreaking features and improvements that redefine the mobile experience and set a new standard for innovation. From a revamped user interface to powerful AI-driven functionalities, iOS 18 represents a significant leap forward in the evolution of Apple's operating system.

One of the most notable enhancements in iOS 18 is the redesigned user interface, which offers a fresh and modern look while retaining the familiar simplicity and elegance that users have come to expect from Apple products. With updated app icons, refined typography, and subtle animations, iOS 18's interface feels more cohesive and polished than ever before, providing a seamless and intuitive user experience across the board.

But it's not just about looks—iOS 18 also introduces several new features and functionalities that enhance productivity, creativity, and convenience. For example, the redesigned Control Center offers quick access to essential settings and controls, making it easier than ever to adjust brightness, volume, and other system preferences on the fly. Additionally, the new Focus mode allows users to customize their device's notification settings based on their current activity or location, helping them stay focused and productive throughout the day.

Another standout feature of iOS 18 is the enhanced Siri experience, which leverages advanced AI algorithms to provide more accurate and contextual responses to user queries. With improved natural language processing capabilities and deeper integration with third-party apps, Siri in iOS 18 is smarter, more versatile, and more helpful than ever before. Whether it's answering questions, setting reminders, or controlling smart home devices, Siri is always ready to assist users in their daily tasks.

Furthermore, iOS 18 introduces several new AI-driven features that take advantage of the device's powerful Neural Engine to deliver personalized and intelligent experiences. For example, the Photos app now offers advanced image recognition and organization capabilities, allowing users to search for photos based on content, location, and other criteria effortlessly. Similarly, the Camera app utilizes AI-driven scene recognition and composition suggestions to help users capture the perfect shot every time.

In addition to these user-facing features, iOS 18 also brings under-the-hood improvements that enhance device performance, security, and privacy. With optimizations for faster app launch times, smoother multitasking, and improved battery life, iOS 18 ensures that users can enjoy a seamless and responsive experience across all their devices. Moreover, enhanced security features such as App Privacy Report and Mail Privacy Protection give users greater control over their data and privacy, ensuring peace of mind in an increasingly connected world.

In summary, iOS 18 represents a significant milestone in the evolution of Apple's operating system, offering a compelling combination of innovative features, refined design, and enhanced performance. With its focus on AI-driven intelligence, user-centric design, and robust security, iOS 18 sets a new standard for mobile computing and reaffirms Apple's commitment to delivering best-in-class experiences to its users.

Major changes in design, user interface, and functionality

In iOS 18, Apple introduces a series of major changes in design, user interface (UI), and functionality that redefine the way users interact with their devices and elevate the overall user experience to new heights. These changes represent a significant departure from previous iterations of iOS, reflecting Apple's ongoing commitment to innovation and user-centric design.

One of the most noticeable changes in iOS 18 is the redesigned user interface, which features a cleaner, more cohesive look that emphasizes clarity, consistency, and ease of use. From updated app icons to refined typography and subtle animations, every aspect of the UI has been meticulously crafted to create a seamless and immersive experience for users.

The Home Screen has undergone a significant revamp, giving users more control over how their apps are organized and displayed. With the ability to create blank spaces, rows, and columns between app icons, users can now personalize their Home Screens to better suit their preferences and workflow, making it easier than ever to find and access their favorite apps.

Furthermore, iOS 18 introduces a new Control Center design that offers quick access to essential settings and controls, such as brightness, volume, and connectivity options. The redesigned Control Center is more intuitive and customizable, allowing users to tailor it to their specific needs and preferences for greater convenience and efficiency.

In addition to these design changes, iOS 18 also introduces several new functionalities that enhance productivity, creativity, and convenience. For example, the new Focus mode allows users to customize their device's notification settings based on their current activity or location, helping them stay focused and productive throughout the day.

Moreover, iOS 18 leverages the power of artificial intelligence (AI) to deliver intelligent and personalized experiences across the system. From enhanced Siri capabilities to AI-driven features in apps like Photos and Camera, iOS 18 harnesses the potential of machine learning to anticipate user needs, streamline workflows, and enhance the overall user experience.

Overall, the major changes in design, UI, and functionality introduced in iOS 18 represent a significant step forward in the evolution of Apple's operating system. With its focus on simplicity, versatility, and intelligence, iOS 18 sets a new standard for mobile computing and reaffirms Apple's commitment to delivering best-in-class experiences to its users.

The significance of AI integration in various aspects of the operating system

The significance of artificial intelligence (AI) integration in various aspects of the iOS 18 operating system cannot be overstated, as it represents a fundamental shift in the way users interact with their devices and the capabilities that these devices offer. AI integration permeates every facet of iOS 18, from intelligent personal assistants to advanced image recognition algorithms, and its impact is felt across the entire user experience.

One of the most significant areas where AI integration is evident is in the evolution of Siri, Apple's virtual assistant. With iOS 18, Siri becomes smarter, more intuitive, and more contextually aware than ever before, thanks to advanced natural language processing capabilities and machine learning algorithms. Users can expect improved conversational abilities, faster and more accurate responses, and deeper integration with third-party apps, making Siri a truly indispensable companion for everyday tasks.

Furthermore, AI integration in iOS 18 extends beyond just Siri to various built-in apps and system functionalities. For example, the Photos app leverages AI algorithms to automatically organize and categorize photos based on content, location, and time, making it easier for users to find and relive their favorite memories. Similarly, the Camera app utilizes AI-driven features such as scene recognition and composition suggestions to help users capture stunning photos effortlessly.

But it's not just about improving existing features—AI integration in iOS 18 also opens up new possibilities for innovation and creativity. With frameworks like Core ML and Create ML, developers can easily integrate AI models into their apps to deliver personalized recommendations, intelligent automation, and immersive experiences tailored to individual user preferences and behaviors. This enables developers to push the boundaries of what's possible in app development and deliver truly transformative experiences to users.

Moreover, AI integration in iOS 18 plays a crucial role in enhancing device performance, efficiency, and security. With features like on-device AI processing and optimization, iOS 18 delivers faster app launch times, smoother multitasking, and improved battery life, ensuring a seamless and responsive user experience across the board. Additionally, AI-driven security features such as App Privacy Report and Mail Privacy Protection give users greater control over their data and privacy, providing peace of mind in an increasingly connected world.

In summary, the significance of AI integration in various aspects of the iOS 18 operating system cannot be overstated. From enhancing user interactions and app functionalities to driving innovation and creativity, AI integration in iOS 18 represents a transformative shift in the way we interact with our devices and the possibilities that these devices offer. As AI continues to evolve and mature, users can expect iOS 18 to deliver even more intelligent, intuitive, and personalized experiences that enrich their lives in meaningful ways.

Chapter 4: Siri: The Ultimate Virtual Assistant

Siri, Apple's virtual assistant, has undergone a remarkable evolution since its introduction, and its transformation in iOS 18 represents a significant leap forward in its capabilities and functionality. From its humble beginnings as a voice-activated assistant to its current status as a sophisticated AI-powered companion, Siri has continually evolved to meet the changing needs and expectations of users.

In iOS 18, Siri undergoes a transformative evolution, leveraging advanced artificial intelligence (AI) algorithms to become smarter, more intuitive, and more contextually aware than ever before. One of the most notable enhancements in iOS 18 is Siri's improved conversational abilities, which enable more natural and fluid interactions with users. Thanks to advanced natural language processing capabilities, Siri in iOS 18 can better understand and interpret user queries, leading to faster and more accurate responses.

Furthermore, Siri's integration with third-party apps is significantly deepened in iOS 18, allowing users to perform a wider range of tasks and access more information than ever before. Whether it's ordering food, booking a ride, or controlling smart home devices, Siri in iOS 18 can seamlessly interact with a growing ecosystem of third-party services, making it a truly indispensable companion for everyday tasks.

But perhaps the most significant transformation of Siri in iOS 18 is its newfound ability to anticipate user needs and provide proactive suggestions and recommendations. Leveraging AI-driven insights and user behavior patterns, Siri in iOS 18 can offer personalized recommendations, reminders, and notifications tailored to individual preferences and habits. Whether it's suggesting nearby restaurants, reminding users to take a break, or notifying them of upcoming events, Siri in iOS 18 becomes a proactive assistant that helps users stay organized, productive, and informed throughout their day.

Moreover, Siri's integration with other system functionalities and apps is enhanced in iOS 18, allowing for deeper and more seamless interactions across the entire operating system. Whether it's sending messages, making calls, or controlling music playback, Siri in iOS 18 can perform a wide range of tasks with just a simple voice command, making it easier than ever for users to access the features and functionalities they need.

In summary, the evolution of Siri in iOS 18 represents a significant milestone in the development of Apple's virtual assistant. With its improved conversational abilities, deeper integration with third-party apps, proactive suggestions, and seamless interactions across the operating system, Siri in iOS 18 becomes a truly indispensable companion that enhances the overall user experience and helps users get more done with their devices. As Siri continues to evolve and mature, users can expect even more exciting developments and enhancements in the future.

The use of large-language models for enhanced natural language understanding

The use of large-language models (LLMs) for enhanced natural language understanding represents a significant breakthrough in the field of artificial intelligence (AI) and has far-reaching implications for various applications and industries. LLMs, such as OpenAI's GPT (Generative Pre-trained Transformer) series and

Google's BERT (Bidirectional Encoder Representations from Transformers), are designed to process and understand natural language at an unprecedented scale, leveraging vast amounts of data and advanced machine learning algorithms to generate contextually relevant responses and insights.

One of the key advantages of LLMs is their ability to capture complex linguistic patterns and nuances, allowing them to understand and generate human-like text with remarkable accuracy and fluency. By training on massive datasets comprising billions of words, sentences, and documents, LLMs can learn intricate relationships between words, phrases, and concepts, enabling them to comprehend and generate natural language with a level of sophistication that was previously unimaginable.

In the context of iOS 18, the use of LLMs for enhanced natural language understanding has several implications for various features and functionalities. For example, Siri, Apple's virtual assistant, can leverage LLMs to improve its conversational abilities, allowing it to understand and respond to user queries in a more contextually relevant and human-like manner. Whether it's answering questions, providing recommendations, or assisting with tasks, Siri in iOS 18 can leverage the power of LLMs to deliver more accurate, informative, and engaging interactions with users.

Furthermore, LLMs can enhance natural language processing (NLP) capabilities across various built-in apps and system functionalities in iOS 18. For example, the Messages app could utilize LLMs to improve auto-complete suggestions and predictive text, making it easier for users to compose messages quickly and accurately. Similarly, the Notes app could leverage LLMs for intelligent note-taking features, such as summarization, categorization, and content generation, helping users organize and manage their notes more effectively.

Moreover, LLMs can enable new AI-driven functionalities and experiences in iOS 18, such as personalized recommendations, predictive analytics, and intelligent automation. By analyzing user behavior, preferences, and context, LLMs can anticipate user needs and provide proactive suggestions and assistance tailored to individual preferences and habits. Whether it's recommending relevant content, predicting user actions, or automating routine tasks, LLMs can enrich the user experience and streamline workflows in iOS 18.

However, it's important to recognize that the use of LLMs also raises ethical and privacy considerations, particularly regarding data privacy, bias, and fairness. As LLMs rely on vast amounts of data to learn and generate text, there is a risk of perpetuating biases and stereotypes present in the training data, leading to potentially harmful outcomes for marginalized communities. Moreover, the sheer scale and complexity of LLMs raise concerns about data privacy and security, as they may inadvertently expose sensitive information or compromise user privacy.

In summary, the use of large-language models for enhanced natural language understanding in iOS 18 represents a significant advancement in AI technology, enabling more accurate, fluent, and contextually relevant interactions with users. By leveraging the power of LLMs, Siri and other built-in apps and functionalities in iOS 18 can deliver more intelligent, personalized, and engaging experiences that enrich the overall user experience. However, it's essential to approach the use of LLMs thoughtfully and responsibly, taking into account ethical, privacy, and security considerations to ensure that the benefits of this technology are realized without compromising user trust and well-being.

In iOS 18, Apple introduces new capabilities to Siri, its virtual assistant, focusing on enhancing conversation abilities and deepening integration with other apps. These improvements represent a significant step forward in making Siri more intuitive, versatile, and seamlessly integrated into users' daily lives.

One of the standout features of Siri in iOS 18 is its improved conversation abilities. Thanks to advancements in natural language processing (NLP) and machine learning algorithms, Siri can now engage in more natural, fluid, and contextually relevant conversations with users. Whether it's answering questions, providing recommendations, or assisting with tasks, Siri in iOS 18 can understand and respond to user queries with greater accuracy and fluency, creating a more immersive and engaging interaction experience.

Furthermore, Siri in iOS 18 boasts deeper integration with other apps and system functionalities, allowing for more seamless and intuitive interactions across the entire operating system. For example, Siri can now perform a wider range of tasks and access more information from third-party apps, enabling users to accomplish more without having to switch between different apps manually. Whether it's ordering food, booking a ride, or controlling smart home devices, Siri in iOS 18 can seamlessly interact with a growing ecosystem of third-party services, making it a truly indispensable companion for everyday tasks.

Moreover, Siri's integration with other system functionalities and apps is enhanced in iOS 18, allowing for deeper and more seamless interactions across the entire operating system. Whether it's sending messages, making calls, or controlling music playback, Siri in iOS 18 can perform a wide range of tasks with just a simple voice command, making it easier than ever for users to access the features and functionalities they need.

Additionally, Siri in iOS 18 benefits from improved privacy and security features, ensuring that users' personal information remains protected at all times. With features like on-device processing and end-to-end encryption, Siri in iOS 18 provides users with peace of mind knowing that their interactions with the virtual assistant are private and secure.

Overall, the new capabilities introduced in Siri in iOS 18 represent a significant advancement in the evolution of Apple's virtual assistant. By focusing on improving conversation abilities and deepening integration with other apps, Apple has made Siri more intuitive, versatile, and seamlessly integrated into users' daily lives, enhancing the overall user experience and making iOS 18 a more powerful and intelligent operating system.

Chapter 5: Redefining User Experience

The impact of iOS 18 on user experience and interaction is profound, as the operating system introduces a host of new features, enhancements, and capabilities that enrich the overall user experience and transform the way users interact with their devices.

One of the key areas where iOS 18 makes a significant impact is in the realm of user interface (UI) design. With its redesigned interface, iOS 18 offers a cleaner, more cohesive, and visually appealing aesthetic that enhances usability and engagement. From updated app icons to refined typography and subtle animations, every aspect of the UI is meticulously crafted to create a seamless and immersive experience for users, making iOS 18 a joy to use and navigate.

Moreover, iOS 18 introduces several new functionalities and enhancements that streamline workflows, boost productivity, and enhance convenience. For example, the revamped Control Center offers quick access to essential settings and controls, while the new Focus mode allows users to customize their device's notification settings based on their current activity or location, helping them stay focused and productive throughout the day.

Furthermore, iOS 18 leverages the power of artificial intelligence (AI) to deliver intelligent and personalized experiences across the system. From enhanced Siri capabilities to AI-driven features in apps like Photos and Camera, iOS 18 harnesses the potential of machine learning to anticipate user needs, streamline workflows, and enhance the overall user experience. Whether it's providing personalized recommendations, automating routine tasks, or delivering proactive suggestions, iOS 18 enriches the user experience by leveraging AI to deliver more intelligent, intuitive, and personalized interactions.

In addition to these enhancements, iOS 18 also introduces improvements in privacy and security, ensuring that users' personal information remains protected at all times. With features like on-device processing and end-to-end encryption, iOS 18 provides users with peace of mind knowing that their data is secure and their privacy is respected, fostering trust and confidence in the platform.

Overall, the impact of iOS 18 on user experience and interaction is overwhelmingly positive, as the operating system introduces a range of new features, enhancements, and capabilities that enrich the overall user experience and elevate the way users interact with their devices. From its redesigned interface to its intelligent AI-driven features, iOS 18 sets a new standard for mobile computing, delivering a seamless, intuitive, and immersive experience that delights users and enhances their everyday lives.

The customizable Home Screen and its implications for users

The introduction of a customizable Home Screen in iOS 18 represents a significant departure from previous iterations of the operating system and has profound implications for users in terms of personalization, organization, and productivity. By giving users more control over the look and layout of their Home Screens, iOS 18 empowers users to tailor their devices to better suit their individual preferences and workflow, enhancing usability and engagement in the process.

One of the most immediate implications of the customizable Home Screen in iOS 18 is the ability for users to personalize their devices in ways that were previously not possible. With the ability to create blank spaces, rows, and columns between app icons, users can now arrange their Home Screens to reflect their unique aesthetic preferences and organizational needs, creating a more visually pleasing and personalized experience.

Moreover, the customizable Home Screen in iOS 18 enables users to organize their apps in a way that makes sense to them, improving accessibility and usability in the process. Whether it's grouping similar apps together, organizing apps by frequency of use, or creating thematic clusters of apps for different activities or contexts, users can now arrange their Home Screens in a way that optimizes efficiency and productivity, making it easier than ever to find and access the apps they need.

Furthermore, the customizable Home Screen in iOS 18 fosters creativity and experimentation, allowing users to explore new ways of interacting with their devices and expressing themselves through customization. From creating custom app layouts and themes to experimenting with different widget configurations and arrangements, users can unleash their creativity and make their devices truly their own, fostering a sense of ownership and personalization that enhances the overall user experience.

Additionally, the customizable Home Screen in iOS 18 has implications for developers, as it opens up new opportunities for app discovery and engagement. With users having more control over the placement and organization of their apps, developers may need to rethink their app design and marketing strategies to ensure that their apps stand out and remain easily accessible to users amidst the sea of customization options.

Overall, the customizable Home Screen in iOS 18 represents a significant evolution in the way users interact with their devices, offering greater flexibility, personalization, and creativity than ever before. By empowering users to customize their devices to better suit their individual preferences and workflow, iOS 18 enhances usability, engagement, and satisfaction, making it easier and more enjoyable for users to harness the full potential of their devices in their everyday lives.

Improvements in app organization, navigation, and accessibility features

In iOS 18, Apple introduces a range of improvements in app organization, navigation, and accessibility features, enhancing the overall user experience and making it easier for users to find, access, and interact with their apps.

App Organization: iOS 18 introduces several enhancements to app organization, allowing users to better organize and manage their apps for improved efficiency and productivity. With the customizable Home Screen, users can now create blank spaces, rows, and columns between app icons, enabling them to arrange their apps in a way that makes sense to them. This flexibility in app layout not only enhances visual aesthetics but also improves accessibility and usability by making it easier for users to locate and access their apps quickly.

Furthermore, iOS 18 introduces improvements to app grouping and categorization, enabling users to group similar apps together into folders or thematic clusters for easier organization. With features like App Library and Smart Stacks, users can declutter their Home Screens and access their apps more efficiently, reducing clutter and simplifying navigation in the process.

Navigation: iOS 18 enhances navigation capabilities, making it easier for users to navigate within and between apps with greater speed and precision. With improvements to gesture-based navigation and multitasking, users can seamlessly switch between apps, access app features, and perform actions with fewer steps and interruptions, enhancing workflow efficiency and productivity.

Additionally, iOS 18 introduces enhancements to system-wide navigation controls, such as the revamped Control Center and redesigned App Switcher, providing users with quicker access to essential settings, controls, and app previews. These improvements streamline navigation and reduce cognitive load, enabling users to focus on the task at hand without being overwhelmed by complex navigation interfaces.

Accessibility Features: iOS 18 introduces a range of accessibility features designed to make the operating system more inclusive and accessible to users with diverse needs and abilities. From enhanced VoiceOver capabilities to new adaptive voice shortcuts, iOS 18 empowers users to customize their devices to better suit their individual preferences and accessibility requirements.

Moreover, iOS 18 introduces improvements to accessibility settings and controls, such as enhanced text-to-speech functionality and customizable font sizes and styles, enabling users to personalize their device experience to accommodate visual, auditory, and motor impairments. These accessibility features ensure that all users, regardless of their abilities, can fully participate in and benefit from the iOS 18 experience.

Overall, the improvements in app organization, navigation, and accessibility features in iOS 18 represent a significant step forward in enhancing the overall user experience and making the operating system more intuitive, efficient, and inclusive. By empowering users to customize their app layouts, navigate their devices with greater ease, and access accessibility features tailored to their needs, iOS 18 ensures that users can get the most out of their devices and enjoy a seamless and enjoyable user experience.

Chapter 6: Enhancements in Built-in Apps

In iOS 18, Apple introduces a range of updates and enhancements to Safari, Apple Maps, Notes, Calendar, and Reminders, offering users new features and improvements that enhance functionality, usability, and overall user experience across these core apps.

Safari: iOS 18 brings significant updates to Safari, Apple's web browser, with an emphasis on improving browsing experience, privacy, and productivity. One of the standout features is the introduction of an "Intelligent Search" option, which uses on-device AI technology to identify key topics and phrases on webpages and offer a summary, making it easier for users to find relevant information quickly.

Additionally, iOS 18 introduces a "Web Eraser" tool in Safari, allowing users to remove unwanted portions of webpages. This feature enables users to customize their browsing experience and focus on the content that matters most to them, enhancing productivity and reducing distractions.

Moreover, Safari in iOS 18 includes an updated quick-access menu available from the address bar, combining page tools and functions currently housed in the Share Sheet. This streamlined interface makes it easier for users to access essential browser features and perform actions with fewer steps, improving usability and efficiency.

Apple Maps: iOS 18 brings several new features and enhancements to Apple Maps, enhancing navigation, exploration, and user experience. One notable addition is support for custom routes, allowing users to input self-selected routes rather than being limited to pre-selected options provided by Apple. This feature gives users greater flexibility and control over their navigation experience, enabling them to choose routes based on their preferences and needs.

Furthermore, iOS 18 introduces the watchOS 10 topographic map feature to the iPhone in Apple Maps, providing users with detailed information about trails, contour lines, elevation, points of interest, and other features useful for hiking and outdoor activities. This enhancement enhances the utility of Apple Maps for outdoor enthusiasts and adventurers, making it easier for them to explore and navigate outdoor environments.

Notes: iOS 18 introduces several updates to the Notes app, enhancing functionality and usability for users who rely on the app for note-taking and organization. One notable addition is support for recording voice memos directly in the app, with recordings embeddable in notes. This feature enables users to capture audio notes quickly and conveniently, enhancing the versatility of the Notes app for capturing ideas, reminders, and other audio content.

Additionally, iOS 18 introduces support for displaying mathematical notation in Notes, allowing users to include a wider range of equations and mathematical expressions in their notes. This enhancement expands the utility of the Notes app for users in academic, scientific, and technical fields, enabling them to create more comprehensive and informative notes with mathematical content.

Calendar and Reminders: iOS 18 brings improvements to the Calendar app, enhancing integration with the Reminders app and introducing new features to streamline task management and organization. One notable addition is Reminders integration in the Calendar app, allowing users to view and interact with reminders directly within the Calendar interface. This enhancement improves task management and organization by providing users with a unified view of their calendar events and reminders, enabling them to plan their schedule more effectively and stay on top of their tasks and commitments.

Overall, the updates and enhancements introduced in Safari, Apple Maps, Notes, Calendar, and Reminders in iOS 18 offer users new features and improvements that enhance functionality, usability, and overall user experience across these core apps. Whether it's improving browsing experience in Safari, enhancing navigation in Apple Maps, adding new features to the Notes app, or streamlining task management in Calendar and Reminders, iOS 18 provides users with tools and capabilities that empower them to do more with their devices and enhance their productivity and efficiency in their daily lives.

iOS 18 introduces several innovative features that enhance productivity, convenience, and user experience across core apps such as Safari, Apple Maps, and Notes. These features leverage artificial intelligence (AI) and advanced algorithms to provide users with intelligent search capabilities, customizable navigation options, and AI-assisted note-taking functionality, revolutionizing how users interact with their devices and access information.

Intelligent Search in Safari: One of the standout features of iOS 18 is the introduction of intelligent search in Safari, Apple's web browser. This feature utilizes on-device AI technology to analyze webpages and identify key topics and phrases, enabling users to access relevant information quickly and efficiently. By offering a summary of the webpage's content, intelligent search in Safari streamlines the browsing experience, allowing users to find answers to their queries without having to read through lengthy articles or pages. Whether it's researching a topic, finding a recipe, or looking up information for work or school, intelligent search in Safari empowers users to access the information they need with just a few taps, enhancing productivity and saving time.

Custom Routes in Apple Maps: iOS 18 introduces the ability to create custom routes in Apple Maps, offering users greater flexibility and control over their navigation experience. With this feature, users can input self-selected routes rather than being limited to pre-selected options provided by Apple. Whether it's planning a scenic drive, avoiding toll roads, or choosing familiar routes, custom routes in Apple Maps enable users to tailor their navigation experience to their preferences and needs, enhancing convenience and personalization. Additionally, custom routes empower users to explore new destinations and discover hidden gems, turning every journey into an adventure.

AI-Assisted Note-Taking in Notes: Another exciting feature introduced in iOS 18 is AI-assisted note-taking in the Notes app. This feature leverages AI technology to enhance the note-taking experience, providing users with intelligent tools and capabilities that streamline the process of capturing and organizing information. For example, AI-assisted note-taking can automatically transcribe voice memos into text, making it easier for users to capture ideas, reminders, and other audio content. Additionally, AI algorithms can analyze the content of notes and provide contextual suggestions and recommendations, such as relevant links, images, or documents, helping users create more comprehensive and informative notes. Whether it's jotting down meeting notes, brainstorming ideas, or keeping track of tasks and deadlines, AI-assisted note-taking in Notes enhances productivity and organization, enabling users to stay focused and efficient.

Overall, the introduction of intelligent search in Safari, custom routes in Apple Maps, and AI-assisted note-taking in Notes represents a significant advancement in iOS 18, offering users new features and capabilities that enhance productivity, convenience, and user experience. By leveraging AI and advanced algorithms, these features empower users to access information quickly and efficiently, navigate with greater flexibility and control, and capture and organize thoughts and ideas effortlessly, making iOS 18 a powerful and indispensable tool for everyday tasks and activities.

The enhancements introduced in iOS 18, including intelligent search in Safari, custom routes in Apple Maps, and AI-assisted note-taking in Notes, have significant implications for user productivity and convenience, revolutionizing how users interact with their devices and access information.

Firstly, the intelligent search feature in Safari streamlines the browsing experience by leveraging AI technology to analyze webpages and provide users with relevant information quickly. This enhancement saves users valuable time and effort by eliminating the need to sift through lengthy articles or pages to find answers to their queries. Whether it's researching a topic for work or school, finding a recipe for dinner, or looking up information on the go, intelligent search in Safari enables users to access the information they need with just a few taps, enhancing productivity and convenience.

Secondly, the introduction of custom routes in Apple Maps offers users greater flexibility and control over their navigation experience, empowering them to tailor their routes to their preferences and needs. This feature enhances convenience by allowing users to avoid traffic congestion, toll roads, or unfamiliar routes, saving time and reducing stress during travel. Whether it's planning a scenic drive, avoiding construction zones, or choosing the fastest route to a destination, custom routes in Apple Maps enable users to navigate with confidence and efficiency, enhancing productivity and convenience on the road.

Lastly, the AI-assisted note-taking feature in Notes enhances productivity and convenience by streamlining the process of capturing and organizing information. By leveraging AI technology to transcribe voice memos into text and provide contextual suggestions and recommendations, this feature simplifies note-taking and helps users stay organized and focused. Whether it's jotting down meeting notes, brainstorming ideas, or keeping track of tasks and deadlines, AI-assisted note-taking in Notes enables users to capture and organize information effortlessly, enhancing productivity and convenience in their daily lives.

Overall, the enhancements introduced in iOS 18 have profound implications for user productivity and convenience, offering users new features and capabilities that streamline tasks, save time, and enhance the overall user experience. By leveraging AI technology and advanced algorithms, these enhancements empower users to access information quickly and efficiently, navigate with greater flexibility and control, and capture and organize thoughts and ideas effortlessly, making iOS 18 a powerful tool for enhancing productivity and convenience in everyday life.

Chapter 7: The Future of Messaging: RCS Integration

The adoption of Rich Communication Services (RCS) in iOS 18 brings significant benefits for iPhone users engaging in conversations with Android users, revolutionizing the messaging experience and bridging the gap between different platforms. RCS represents a modernized and more feature-rich alternative to traditional SMS/MMS messaging, offering a range of advantages for cross-platform communication:

1. Enhanced Messaging Experience: RCS introduces a variety of features that go beyond the capabilities of traditional SMS/MMS, such as support for higher resolution photos and videos, larger file sizes, and file sharing. These enhancements enrich the messaging experience, allowing users to share multimedia content with higher quality and greater convenience.

2. Improved Group Chats: With RCS, group chats between iPhone and Android users benefit from

better performance and additional features. Features like cross-platform emoji reactions, real-time typing indicators, and read receipts enhance the interactivity and engagement of group conversations, making them more enjoyable and efficient for all participants.

3. Seamless Communication: RCS enables seamless communication between iPhone and Android users, eliminating the barriers and limitations imposed by traditional SMS/MMS messaging. Users can exchange messages, photos, videos, and other content effortlessly, regardless of the platform they are using, fostering closer connections and more meaningful interactions.

4. Cost-Free Messaging Over Wi-Fi: One of the key benefits of RCS is the ability to send messages over Wi-Fi, in addition to cellular networks. This means that users can send RCS messages without incurring additional charges, making it a cost-effective option for communication,

especially in areas with limited or expensive cellular data coverage.

5. Compatibility and Interoperability: RCS ensures compatibility and interoperability between different messaging platforms and devices, allowing users to communicate seamlessly across iOS and Android ecosystems. This interoperability breaks down the barriers between different platforms and fosters greater inclusivity and accessibility in communication.

Overall, the adoption of RCS in iOS 18 brings significant benefits for iPhone users engaging in conversations with Android users, offering an enhanced messaging experience, improved group chats, seamless communication, cost-free messaging over Wi-Fi, and compatibility and interoperability across platforms. With RCS, iPhone users can enjoy a more feature-rich and versatile messaging experience when communicating with friends, family, and colleagues using Android devices, fostering closer connections and more meaningful interactions across different platforms.

The implications of improved cross-platform communication for users

The improved cross-platform communication facilitated by features like RCS in iOS 18 has profound implications for users, revolutionizing the way people communicate and interact with each other across different platforms. These implications extend to various aspects of users' lives, including social connections, productivity, accessibility, and convenience:

1. Enhanced Social Connections: Improved cross-platform communication fosters closer connections and stronger relationships among users by enabling seamless communication across different devices and platforms. Whether it's staying in touch with friends and family members who use Android devices or collaborating with colleagues and classmates who

use different operating systems, users can maintain meaningful connections and engage in more frequent and interactive communication, regardless of the devices they are using.

2. Increased Productivity: The ability to communicate seamlessly across platforms enhances productivity by streamlining collaboration, coordination, and information sharing among users. With features like RCS enabling enhanced group chats, file sharing, and real-time collaboration, users can work more efficiently, coordinate tasks more effectively, and access information more quickly, leading to improved productivity and workflow efficiency in both personal and professional contexts.

3. Greater Accessibility: Improved cross-platform communication enhances accessibility by breaking down barriers and enabling more inclusive and accessible communication experiences for users with diverse needs and abilities. Features like RCS ensure compatibility and interoperability across different platforms,

allowing users to communicate seamlessly regardless of the devices they are using. This inclusivity ensures that all users, regardless of their device preferences or accessibility requirements, can fully participate in and benefit from cross-platform communication, fostering greater accessibility and inclusivity in digital communication.

4. Enhanced Convenience: Improved cross-platform communication offers users greater convenience and flexibility in how they communicate and interact with others. With features like RCS enabling cost-free messaging over Wi-Fi and support for higher resolution photos and videos, users can communicate more affordably and conveniently, regardless of their location or data plan. Additionally, features like real-time typing indicators and cross-platform emoji reactions enhance the interactivity and engagement of conversations, making communication more enjoyable and efficient for all participants.

Overall, the implications of improved cross-platform communication for users are far-reaching, encompassing social connections, productivity, accessibility, and convenience. By enabling seamless communication across different platforms, features like RCS in iOS 18 empower users to maintain closer connections, work more efficiently, access information more easily, and communicate more affordably and conveniently, enhancing the overall communication experience and enriching the ways in which people connect and interact with each other in the digital age.

Chapter 8: Accessibility and Inclusivity

iOS 18 introduces a range of new accessibility features designed to make the operating system more inclusive and accessible to users with diverse needs and abilities. These features build upon Apple's commitment to accessibility and aim to empower users to customize their devices to better suit their individual preferences and accessibility requirements. Some of the new accessibility features introduced in iOS 18 include:

1. Adaptive Voice Shortcuts: iOS 18 introduces Adaptive Voice Shortcuts, a feature that enables users to create custom voice commands linked to specific accessibility settings. Users can create a custom phrase and then select an accessibility setting to activate when the phrase is spoken. This feature enhances accessibility by providing users with a convenient way to toggle accessibility features such as VoiceOver, Voice Control, Zoom, and more, using voice commands, making it easier for users to access and control accessibility

settings without needing to navigate through menus or settings.

2. Live Speech Categories: iOS 18 enhances the Live Speech feature, which provides real-time speech recognition for users with speech impairments, by introducing user-created categories. Users can create custom categories to organize their Live Speech phrases based on their preferences and needs, making it easier to access and use the feature. This enhancement improves the usability and customization options of Live Speech, allowing users to tailor the feature to their specific communication requirements and preferences.

3. Improved Text-to-Speech Functionality: iOS 18 includes improvements to text-to-speech functionality, enhancing the accessibility of content for users with visual impairments or reading difficulties. The improved text-to-speech functionality offers more natural-sounding voices, improved pronunciation accuracy, and enhanced support for different languages and accents,

ensuring that text-based content is more accessible and easier to understand for all users.

4. Customizable Font Sizes and Styles: iOS 18 introduces new customization options for font sizes and styles, allowing users to personalize the appearance of text on their devices to better suit their visual preferences and needs. Users can adjust the size and style of system fonts, app text, and interface elements, making it easier to read and interact with content on the screen. This customization feature enhances accessibility by enabling users to customize their device's display to meet their individual vision requirements and preferences, improving readability and usability for users with visual impairments or preferences for specific font styles.

Overall, the new accessibility features introduced in iOS 18 aim to make the operating system more inclusive and accessible to users with diverse needs and abilities. By providing enhanced customization options, improved voice command functionality, and better support for speech recognition and text-to-speech, iOS 18 empowers users to tailor their device experience to their individual accessibility requirements and preferences, ensuring that all users can fully participate in and benefit from the iOS ecosystem.

The Adaptive Voice Shortcuts, Live Speech improvements, and other accessibility enhancements

In iOS 18, Apple introduces several accessibility enhancements aimed at improving the overall accessibility and inclusivity of the operating system for users with diverse needs and abilities. These enhancements include the introduction of Adaptive Voice Shortcuts, improvements to the Live Speech feature, and other accessibility enhancements that empower users to customize their devices and access features more easily.

1. Adaptive Voice Shortcuts: Adaptive Voice Shortcuts is a new feature introduced in iOS 18

that allows users to create custom voice commands linked to specific accessibility settings. With Adaptive Voice Shortcuts, users can create a custom phrase and then select an accessibility setting to activate when the phrase is spoken. For example, users can create a voice command to toggle VoiceOver, Voice Control, Zoom, or other accessibility features, making it easier to access and control these features using voice commands. Adaptive Voice Shortcuts enhance accessibility by providing users with a convenient and efficient way to access and activate accessibility settings, reducing the need to navigate through menus or settings manually.

2. Live Speech Improvements: iOS 18 includes enhancements to the Live Speech feature, which provides real-time speech recognition for users with speech impairments. The improvements to Live Speech include the introduction of user-created categories, allowing users to organize their Live Speech phrases based on their preferences and needs. This enhancement

improves the usability and customization options of Live Speech, enabling users to tailor the feature to their specific communication requirements. Additionally, iOS 18 includes improvements to text-to-speech functionality, offering more natural-sounding voices, improved pronunciation accuracy, and enhanced support for different languages and accents. These improvements ensure that text-based content is more accessible and easier to understand for users with visual impairments or reading difficulties, enhancing the overall accessibility of the operating system.

3. Other Accessibility Enhancements: In addition to Adaptive Voice Shortcuts and Live Speech improvements, iOS 18 introduces other accessibility enhancements aimed at improving the overall accessibility and usability of the operating system. These enhancements include customizable font sizes and styles, allowing users to personalize the appearance of text on their devices to better suit their visual preferences and needs. iOS 18 also includes improvements to

accessibility features such as VoiceOver, Voice Control, and Zoom, enhancing their functionality and usability for users with diverse needs and abilities. These accessibility enhancements empower users to customize their devices and access features more easily, ensuring that all users can fully participate in and benefit from the iOS ecosystem.

Overall, the accessibility enhancements introduced in iOS 18 demonstrate Apple's continued commitment to making its products accessible and inclusive for users with diverse needs and abilities. By introducing features like Adaptive Voice Shortcuts, improving Live Speech functionality, and enhancing other accessibility features, iOS 18 ensures that all users can access and use their devices with ease, regardless of their individual accessibility requirements or preferences.

Apple's unwavering commitment to inclusivity and empowerment through technology is deeply rooted in its core values and has been a driving force behind the company's innovations and initiatives since its inception. From the design of its products to its corporate culture and social responsibility efforts, Apple has consistently demonstrated its dedication to creating a more inclusive and equitable world through technology.

At the heart of Apple's commitment to inclusivity is its inclusive design philosophy, which places accessibility and usability at the forefront of product development. Apple designs its products with the understanding that diversity is a strength and that technology should be accessible to all users, regardless of their abilities or backgrounds. This philosophy is evident in the intuitive and user-friendly design of Apple products, which prioritize simplicity, clarity, and ease of use for everyone.

One of the most tangible expressions of Apple's commitment to inclusivity is its extensive array of accessibility features built into its products and services. These features are designed to empower users with disabilities to fully participate in and benefit from the digital world. From VoiceOver, which provides spoken descriptions of on-screen content for users with visual impairments, to Switch Control, which enables users with mobility impairments to control their devices using adaptive switches, Apple's accessibility features are integral to its mission of inclusivity and empowerment.

Apple also actively promotes diversity and inclusion within its workforce and the broader tech industry through various initiatives and programs. The company has implemented diversity and inclusion training programs, established employee resource groups, and partnered with external organizations to support underrepresented groups in tech. Additionally, Apple has launched initiatives such as the Apple Developer Academy and the App Store

Entrepreneur Camp to provide education, mentorship, and support to aspiring developers and entrepreneurs from diverse backgrounds.

Furthermore, Apple is committed to corporate responsibility and ethical business practices that prioritize social and environmental sustainability. The company has made significant investments in renewable energy, environmental conservation, and supply chain transparency to minimize its impact on the planet and promote sustainable development. Apple's commitment to corporate responsibility extends to its support for education, environmental conservation, and human rights advocacy, reflecting its belief in using technology as a force for positive change in the world.

In summary, Apple's commitment to inclusivity and empowerment through technology is evident in every aspect of its business, from product design and accessibility features to diversity initiatives and corporate responsibility efforts. By prioritizing accessibility, diversity, and social impact, Apple seeks to create a more inclusive, equitable, and sustainable world for all.

Chapter 9: The Road Ahead

Speculating on the future of iOS and mobile computing involves considering current trends, technological advancements, and emerging challenges to envision how these technologies may evolve in the years to come. While the future is inherently uncertain, several potential developments can be anticipated based on current trajectories and ongoing innovation in the tech industry.

1. Enhanced Artificial Intelligence Integration: Artificial intelligence (AI) is likely to play an increasingly prominent role in the future of iOS and mobile computing. As AI technologies continue to advance, we can expect to see deeper integration of AI capabilities into iOS devices, enabling more intelligent and personalized user experiences. This may include AI-powered assistants that anticipate user needs, enhanced natural language processing for seamless

interactions, and intelligent automation features that streamline tasks and workflows.
2. Augmented Reality (AR) and Mixed Reality (MR) Experiences: AR and MR technologies are poised to transform the way we interact with mobile devices and the world around us. In the future, iOS devices may support more sophisticated AR and MR experiences, blurring the lines between the digital and physical worlds. From immersive gaming and entertainment to practical applications in fields like education, healthcare, and retail, AR and MR have the potential to revolutionize mobile computing and unlock new possibilities for creativity, collaboration, and productivity.
3. Continued Focus on Privacy and Security: As the digital landscape becomes increasingly complex and interconnected, privacy and security will remain paramount concerns for iOS and mobile computing. Apple is likely to continue prioritizing user privacy and security by implementing robust encryption, stringent data

protection measures, and transparent privacy controls. Additionally, advancements in biometric authentication, secure hardware components, and privacy-preserving technologies may further enhance the security of iOS devices and safeguard user data against emerging threats and vulnerabilities.

4. Convergence of Mobile and Wearable Technologies: The convergence of mobile and wearable technologies is expected to accelerate in the future, blurring the boundaries between smartphones, smartwatches, and other connected devices. iOS devices may seamlessly integrate with wearable gadgets, such as augmented reality glasses, health monitoring devices, and smart accessories, to deliver more cohesive and immersive experiences. This convergence may enable new forms of interaction, communication, and productivity, empowering users to stay connected and productive wherever they go.

5. Advancements in User Interface and Interaction Paradigms: The future of iOS and mobile computing may witness significant advancements in user interface (UI) and interaction paradigms, driven by innovations in gesture-based controls, voice commands, haptic feedback, and contextual awareness. iOS devices may adopt more intuitive and immersive UI designs that adapt to user preferences and behavior, making interactions more natural and seamless. Additionally, advancements in display technologies, such as foldable screens and flexible displays, may open up new possibilities for multi-modal interaction and content consumption on mobile devices.

Overall, the future of iOS and mobile computing holds exciting possibilities for innovation, creativity, and transformation. By embracing emerging technologies, addressing evolving user needs, and upholding principles of privacy, security, and inclusivity, iOS is poised to continue shaping the future of mobile computing and redefining the way we engage with technology in our daily lives.

Potential developments in AI, machine learning, and mobile technology

As we look toward the future, the convergence of AI, machine learning, and mobile technology presents a landscape ripe with possibilities and innovations. These fields are poised to intersect in increasingly profound ways, reshaping the way we interact with and utilize mobile devices in our daily lives.

One potential development lies in the realm of personalized experiences. AI algorithms, fueled by vast amounts of data, have the potential to tailor mobile experiences to individual users with unprecedented precision. From personalized recommendations for apps, content, and services to adaptive user interfaces that evolve based on user behavior, the integration of AI and machine learning promises to usher in a new era of hyper-personalization in mobile technology.

Moreover, advancements in AI-driven natural language processing (NLP) and conversational interfaces are likely to redefine the way we interact with our devices. Virtual assistants and chatbots powered by sophisticated AI algorithms will become more adept at understanding context, intent, and nuance, enabling more natural and seamless communication between humans and machines. This could lead to a future where voice commands, text-based interactions, and even gestures serve as intuitive means of engaging with mobile devices, enhancing accessibility and usability for users across diverse demographics.

In addition to improving user experiences, AI and machine learning are poised to revolutionize mobile app development and optimization. Developers will increasingly rely on AI-driven tools and frameworks to automate tasks such as code generation, testing, and performance optimization, accelerating the pace of innovation and reducing time-to-market for new apps and features. Furthermore, AI-powered analytics and insights will enable developers to gain deeper understanding of user behavior, preferences, and trends, empowering them to create more compelling and impactful mobile experiences.

Looking ahead, we can also anticipate advancements in AI-enhanced imaging and augmented reality (AR) experiences on mobile devices. AI algorithms will play a crucial role in enhancing image quality, enabling real-time object recognition, and supporting immersive AR applications. From AI-driven camera features that enhance photography to AR experiences that seamlessly blend digital content with the physical world, the integration of AI and machine learning will unlock new creative possibilities and enrich the mobile user experience.

Overall, the future of AI, machine learning, and mobile technology holds tremendous promise for innovation and advancement. By harnessing the power of AI-driven insights, automation, and personalization, mobile devices will become even more indispensable tools for communication, productivity, and entertainment, shaping the way we live, work, and interact with the world around us.

As we embark on this journey into the future of technology, it's essential to embrace the possibilities that lie ahead with a sense of optimism, curiosity, and open-mindedness. The rapid pace of innovation in AI, machine learning, and mobile technology presents us with a wealth of opportunities to enrich our lives, enhance our experiences, and shape the world around us in profound ways.

By embracing the possibilities of future innovations, we empower ourselves to adapt, evolve, and thrive in an ever-changing digital landscape. Whether it's leveraging AI-driven personalization to tailor our mobile experiences to our individual preferences, embracing conversational interfaces to communicate more intuitively with our devices, or exploring the creative potential of AR-enhanced imaging and immersive experiences, the future offers endless avenues for exploration and discovery.

Moreover, by embracing innovation, we become active participants in shaping the future of technology and its impact on society. As we harness the power of AI, machine learning, and mobile technology to address pressing challenges, such as accessibility, sustainability, and social equity, we have the opportunity to create a more inclusive, equitable, and sustainable world for all.

So, let us embrace the possibilities of future innovations with enthusiasm, curiosity, and a spirit of collaboration. Let us embrace the unknown with an open heart and an open mind, knowing that the journey ahead is filled with boundless potential and endless opportunities for growth, discovery, and positive change. Together, let us embark on this journey into the future with optimism, courage, and a shared sense of purpose, as we shape the world of tomorrow today.

Conclusion

In conclusion, our exploration of the future of technology, particularly focusing on the advancements in iOS 18's AI capabilities, has revealed a landscape rich with possibilities and opportunities for innovation. Throughout this book, we have delved into the integration of artificial intelligence, machine learning, and mobile technology, highlighting key developments and potential implications for users and society as a whole.

iOS 18 represents a significant milestone in the evolution of mobile computing, with its groundbreaking AI advancements poised to revolutionize the way we interact with our devices. From personalized experiences and conversational interfaces to AI-driven automation and augmented reality, iOS 18's AI capabilities hold the promise of transforming our mobile experiences in profound ways.

At the heart of iOS 18's AI advancements lies the potential to empower users, enhance accessibility, and foster greater inclusion and equity in the digital realm. By harnessing the power of AI-driven insights, automation, and personalization, iOS 18 opens up new possibilities for creativity, productivity, and connectivity, empowering users to unleash their full potential and embrace the transformative power of technology in their lives.

As we reflect on the significance of iOS 18's AI advancements, we are reminded of the importance of embracing innovation, curiosity, and open-mindedness in our relationship with technology. By exploring and embracing the potential of AI, machine learning, and mobile technology, we can unlock new opportunities for growth, discovery, and positive change in our lives and communities.

In closing, let us embrace the possibilities of future innovations with enthusiasm, curiosity, and a sense of adventure. Let us harness the power of technology to create a brighter, more inclusive, and sustainable future for all. Together, let us embark on this journey into the future with optimism, courage, and a shared commitment to shaping a world where technology serves as a force for good, enriching our lives and enhancing our collective well-being.

www.ingramcontent.com/pod-product-compliance
Lightning Source LLC
Chambersburg PA
CBHW050234230526
45470CB00005B/1939